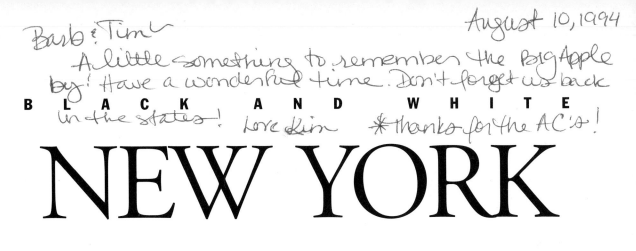

Barb & Tim August 10, 1994
A little something to remember the Big Apple by! Have a wonderful time. Don't forget us back in the states! Love Kim *thanks for the AC's!

BLACK AND WHITE

NEW YORK

TEXT: BILL HARRIS

PHOTO EDITOR: LESLIE FRATKIN

SERIES EDITOR: J.C. SUARÈS

THOMASSON-GRANT

Published by
Thomasson-Grant, Inc.

Copyright © 1994
Thomasson-Grant.
Text copyright © 1994
Bill Harris.

Printed in Hong Kong

ISBN 1-56566-061-7

00 99 98 97 96 95 94
5 4 3 2 1

Inquiries should be
directed to:
Thomasson-Grant, Inc.
One Morton Drive,
Suite 500
Charlottesville, Virginia
22903-6806
(804) 977-1780

Facing page

**The Brooklyn Bridge wasn't
the world's first suspension
bridge; that honor belongs**
to the one over Menai
Strait in Wales. It wasn't
the first for designer
George Washington
Roebling, either. He had
been spinning cables for
bridges for more than a
quarter century before
turning to what he called
"the Great East River
Bridge." But when it was
finished in 1883, the Brooklyn Bridge was the world's
largest suspension bridge,
with Gothic towers taller
than any structure in
New York and four mas-
sive steel cables holding up
a roadway high enough, at
119 feet above the water,
to allow tall-masted ships
to pass beneath it. Few
bridges are as inspiring to
photographers as Roebling's
masterpiece.

Jack Finney's novel *Time and Again* is near the top of everyone's list of favorite books about New York. It involves time travel, an unsolved mystery, a love story, and a fascinating look at the New York of the 1880s. For those of us who lead neighborhood tours, it is a natural platform for any number of excursions that give us an opportunity to show off for our neighbors as well as for out-of-towners.

Several years ago, I dipped into the book for a walking-tour-with-a-difference along Fifth Avenue. I followed the path of Finney's hero, Si Morley, who was transported back to January 23, 1882 and recorded his impressions of a horsecar ride downtown from 59th Street.

The avenue itself was tree-lined back then, and in the shade of the trees among elegant mansions, he passed St. Luke's Hospital at West 54th Street, which was replaced by the University Club in 1899. St. Patrick's Cathedral was where it belonged, although its towers were still in the future, but across 50th Street, where Saks ought to have been, was the Buckingham Hotel. Below it, on both sides, an endless row of brownstones stretched as far as the eye could see, interspersed with more hotels, at least one country inn, a few markets, and a butchershop. The ride ended at 42nd Street, where he found the Public Library's space filled with the Croton Reservoir behind massive walls higher than anything in sight except the Cathedral eight blocks uptown.

Morley's 1882 tour took him past the Catholic Orphan Asylum, but in the city he knew, the 51st Street corner was the site of the Best & Co. department store. Mine found Olympic Tower there. And if we repeated the tour today, we'd have to account for the Warner Bros. store, Trump Tower, and Takashimaya, none of which existed in 1970. We'd have to explain what happened to the bronze traffic lights with little statues on top, how the Gotham Hotel got to be known as the Peninsula, when the Arnold Constable store became a branch of the Library, why Bendel's moved around the corner from 57th Street, and what ever became of its neighbor, Bonwit Teller. The retail scene is constantly changing, of course, but we like to think we'll never forget old favorites.

One of the basic rules of giving walking tours is to take the walk in advance to make sure that there are no surprises around the next corner. Even landmarked districts like Greenwich Village are constantly changing, and nothing diminishes a guide's credibility more than to be forced to say "this wasn't here a week ago." The ultimate question is always "what was?" Most New Yorkers know that the Empire State Building is on the site of the original Waldorf-Astoria, but how many remember that the Singer Tower was right across Liberty Street from the site of the World Trade Center up until 1970, when it became the tallest building ever torn down?

Fortunately for New Yorkers who love this place, photographers have been preserving the cityscape almost from the day the art was invented in 1839. And many of them consider themselves historians as well as artists. Sid Kaplan is one of them. He says his interest in photography began with a teen-age crush on his hometown that was fueled by a weekly feature in the Sunday News that ran comparative photographs of a different city block each week, showing how it looked then and fifty years earlier. "It blew me away," he says, "that the streets never looked the same. And I knew they would change again. Photography was, to my mind, the only way to preserve a city that is constantly changing." That was in the early 1950s, and Kaplan has been recording the change ever since.

Harvey Wang's photographic career began with an admiration for the classic images of the New York of the 1930s and 1940s, and it was only natural for him to work in the same tradition, which led him to an interesting discovery. Although he is too young to remember many of the scenes photographed by the likes of Andreas Feininger, Lewis Hine, Berenice Abbott, Margaret Bourke-White, and Walker Evans, his camera has shown him that the substructure is always there in spite of cosmetic change. This is his chief reason for preferring black and white. "It is the only medium capable of bringing it to the surface," he says. "This is a vibrant city, and black and white images of it help to tame the vibrancy so we can see what is really there." He also notes that the East-West layout of New York's crosstown streets follows the path of the sun, presenting a constantly changing play of light and shadow and providing a unique mood that only black and white film can capture.

But there is more to it than capturing a mood. The camera also freezes moments in time. Not long after photography was invented, an English writer proclaimed that ". . . thus are incidents of time, and the forms of space, simultaneously recorded, and every picture becomes an authentic chapter in the history of the world." And in spite of technicians whose computers can alter an image pixel by pixel, even the most sophisticated among us still believe that the camera does not lie, or, as a newspaper announcing the birth of photography put it, "we can hardly accuse the sun of having an imagination."

Fortunately, we *do* have an imagination, and not many things excite it quite as much as conjuring up our own images of the New York that existed a year ago, a decade ago, a half-century ago—enhanced by the art of photographers who love this city as much as we do.

Pages 8-9

On July 27, 1956, the Swedish-American liner *Stockholm* returned to New York with a forty-foot hole in her bow after having collided two nights earlier with the *Andrea Doria*, the pride of the Italian line, off the coast of Nantucket. Of the nearly 1,700 passengers aboard the two vessels, over 70 lost their lives. The *Andrea Doria* sank to the bottom in 250 feet of water. Among the survivors was 14-year-old Linda Morgan, who was catapulted by the collision, still asleep, from her bunk aboard the Italian ship to the deck of the *Stockholm*, where she was awakened by a kitchen steward.

Back before jumbo jets whisked travelers in and out of New York, the Douglas DC-3 was the workhorse that did the job. It represented the latest word in transportation when photographer G. Enell stopped this one in its path over midtown Manhattan. At that moment, the flight attendant (a "stewardess" in those days) was probably asking the passengers to fasten their seatbelts and extinguish all smoking materials. But then, as now, their minds weren't on safety or comfort so much as on squirming in their seats to get a better view of the greatest diorama ever created by man.

Facing page
The Cunard liner *Queen Mary* carried 2,000 passengers at a time on round trips between Southampton, England, and New York from 1936 until her retirement in 1967 to Long Beach, California. Every arrival was a dramatic event, including this one recorded in 1950 by Andreas Feininger. The *Queen Mary* and her sister ship the *Queen Elizabeth* were berthed at a West 50th Street pier for several months in 1939—refugees from the war in Europe. The *Queen Mary* was eventually painted dull gray and turned into a troop ship making weekly runs from New York to Gaurock, Scotland, during the build-up to D-Day.

The Republicans have never convened in New York, but elephants have been appearing at Madison Square Garden every year since the original Garden was built in 1890. Although Barnum & Bailey doesn't usually bring donkeys on its train, it does offer a nicely decorated "reasonable facsimile." And the parade from the Sunnyside railroad yard in Queens to the Garden is much more fun than any political convention.

Facing page
On November 9, 1965, right in the middle of the evening rush hour, the lights suddenly went out in eight northeastern states and parts of southeastern Canada. For certain home-bound New Yorkers, the outage added the inconvenience of darkness, as straphangers found the subways stopped dead in their tracks. But scratch a New Yorker and you'll find a pedestrian—once flashlight-equipped police officers arrived to light their way, the passengers marched single file out to the street as though nothing had happened, proving once again that nobody handles a disaster with more aplomb than a New Yorker.

When the Third Avenue El began operating in 1878, there were nine stations below 9th Street, the southernmost stop on Third Avenue. These included one at Fulton Street, where the route ran northward over Pearl Street. Todd Webb was intrigued by the 1946 cityscape from the station's platform, but photographing it turned out to be a challenge: "The platform seemed to be constantly shaking," he said, "and it took some luck to get a sharp image." Had he been there a few decades earlier, he'd have faced a much different problem: until the summer of 1902, all the trains on the El were pulled by steam locomotives.

Facing page
Who says you can't find a cab when it rains? Todd Webb found lots of them on Sixth Avenue one rainy day back in 1946, but not one of them had its dome light lit as a signal that it was available. But such frustrations are among the things New Yorkers love to grumble about. In recent years, the loudest complaints center around cab drivers who don't speak English and don't know the city. But like the rainy-day mutterings, the situation goes back to the first motorized taxis that appeared on the streets in 1907, and even before, when cabs were all horse-drawn. From the earliest times, hacking has been an equal-opportunity occupation, offering new immigrants the opportunity for an honest dollar.

When the United Nations Secretariat Building was built, its all-glass side walls prompted critics to predict that it would be so hard to keep cool on sunny days, it would become obsolete after just one summer. That was more than forty years ago. Today, the building is surrounded by dozens of glass-walled neighbors. Although the UN revolutionized the art of building skyscrapers, the windows are still kept clean the old-fashioned way—with a sponge and a squeegee—and, quite possibly, a lump in the throat of the man in the harness.

Facing page
When the Chrysler Building went up in 1930, auto magnate Walter Chrysler authorized the addition of a 123-foot spire to make it the world's tallest structure, hoping to create a lasting memorial to himself. But less than a year later, structural ironworkers at the Empire State Building boasted a higher perch and couldn't help rubbing it in. Many of the

images of the Empire State construction were captured by Lewis Hine, who followed the progress of the 300 ironworkers from a specially-designed basket that allowed him to swing out from the building. Hine was in awe of the "sky boys who ride the ball to the 90th floor or higher and defy death to the staccato chattering of a pneumatic riveting hammer."

The Chrysler Building is the favorite of many New Yorkers. But few of them have ever seen its fantastic gargoyles up close except in the photographs taken by Margaret Bourke-White in 1934. The images made the photographer as famous as the building, but people were forced to guess how she captured them. Fortunately, Oscar Graubner was up there too, and provided us with this proof that she didn't use a telephoto lens. This particular stainless steel bird is perched on the building's northwest corner. The structure in the background is the former RCA Building, now called the GE Building, which was less than a year old at the time.

Even youngsters who never saw the movie know that King Kong was the most famous visitor ever to reach the top of the Empire State Building, even though the list has included kings and queens and real-life movie stars. In 1983, to mark the 50th anniversary of the great ape's first visit, a huge replica appeared on the mooring mast (so-named because it was originally intended to moor dirigibles), only to fall victim to gusty winds within a matter of hours. But before the plastic Kong was blown away, Sid Kaplan managed to record its brief appearance for those who missed the party.

Facing page
On July 28, 1945, an Army B-25 bomber flying in heavy fog crashed into the north side of the Empire State Building at the 79th floor, 913 feet above 34th Street. Fourteen people were killed and twenty-six injured, a toll that would surely have been higher had it not been a Saturday morning. The plane's wings were sheared off, and one of its engines was forced out the other side of the building, landing on a 33rd Street rooftop. The other engine plunged down an elevator shaft, and 800 gallons of flaming gasoline poured down the stairwells. A large piece of the plane remained wedged in an eighteen-by-twenty-foot hole in the side of the building. It took a year for repair crews to completely restore the building. Except for the hole, one badly bent steel beam, and some heavy water and fire damage, the building took the blow in stride.

The photographer known as Weegee went up to the Empire State Building Observatories one fine day in 1950, but, as was typical of him, he wasn't interested in traditional views of the city. In his mind, the city wasn't a collection of buildings, but an even more fascinating collection of people, and thanks to a sudden gust of wind, his search for human drama gave us this little tableau, which one might say constitutes an urban love story. It's still windy up there on the 102nd floor, but styles have changed, and capricious winds are no longer as likely to reveal as much as they did back then.

Facing page
In the comic books as well as in the movies, if Lois Lane and Perry White and Jimmy Olsen didn't know Superman's true identity as mild-mannered reporter Clark Kent, we did. And we also knew where the Man of Steel spent his time when he wasn't flexing his muscles on the edges of rooftops: Gotham City's secret identity was New York, of course. What other city could contain such a hero?

**The last elevated railroad
to serve Manhattan was
torn down in 1955, as Sid**
Kaplan recorded in this
image of the last days of
the Chatham Square
station. The Third Avenue
El was Manhattan's first
elevated line, beginning in
1878 with service between
South Ferry and Chatham
Square at the edge of Chinatown. Within another
twenty years, the line had
extended into the Bronx,
and by the time the demo-
lition crews reached
Chatham Square, the
station had also been
connected to City Hall by a
spur line added to the El's
three tracks, making it one
of the city's busiest stops.

Facing page
**Back in the 1920s, flag-
pole-sitting was a popular
way to attract the attention**
of the tabloid press, but
few people were
impressed by the guys
who made their living
painting flagpoles. This
particular pole, one of a

pair at the edge of the roof
of Grand Central Terminal
flanking the clock that
faces 42nd Street, is no
longer there. But there is
still plenty of work for pole
painters all over town.
The façade in the back-
ground is the Hotel Com-
modore, one of eight
hotels built on the proper-
ty of the New York
Central Railroad after the

terminal opened in 1913.
Its exterior was covered
over with metal and glass
when it became the Grand
Hyatt. Of the eight hotels,
three have been demol-
ished, and like the
Commodore, the Biltmore,
once on Madison Avenue at
43rd Street, has been
altered beyond recognition.

Pages 26-27

As much as everyone loves her, the Brooklyn Bridge was almost completely neglected for nearly a century until the late 1970s, when a massive $105.4-million renovation was begun. These workers, photographed by Chaim Kanner, are still involved in the project, which is scheduled to be completed in 1995. Part of the job has been to replace all of the suspenders from the cables to the deck. The engineers carefully cut the old ones into short lengths, which were sold as souvenirs at $50 apiece, raising $25 million toward the cost of the project.

Pages 28-29

Visitors to the Admiral George Dewey Promenade at the edge of Battery Park are usually drawn to look out at the Statue of Liberty and Ellis Island. But some, like this little girl photographed by Flo Fox, are more intrigued by the pigeons. Not far from this spot is the massive East Coast War Memorial with a huge bronze eagle staring out at the seascape. When it was unveiled in 1961, sculptor Albino Manca confessed that his inspiration for the bird came from the pigeons he studied on the sidewalks of New York.

Facing page

The five-story cast-iron building at Broadway and 10th Street was built in 1862 for A. T. Stewart as the world's first—and for years its most elegant—department store. It became Wanamaker's in 1896 and survived until 1952. The building was demolished in 1956, but not before it was gutted in a spectacular fire that raged for several days. The fire brought apparatus and 300 men, of whom about a third were treated for injuries, from 33 fire companies. New York's fire department is divided into 422 companies with 10,500 firefighters and officers, known as New York's Bravest.

Although the city was once considered a great melting pot of the world's cultures, New York's tradition of celebrating individual heritages has saved it from a complete meltdown. Among the groups that cling tenaciously to their roots are the Hasidim, a Jewish sect founded in eighteenth-century Poland. Although their lives are centered on strict devotion to tradition and prayer, joy is at the heart of their religious belief, which is why scenes such as this one, captured by Chaim Kanner, are common in Brooklyn's Hasidic neighborhoods.

Facing page
According to the old song, kids play ring-around-the-rosy on the sidewalks of New York. They still do, although maybe not in quite the same way as these kids, who were cooling off one summer day in 1946 when Todd Webb photographed them. Although there are parks and playgrounds in virtually every New York neighborhood, the so-called "mean streets" are still filled with fun for youngsters who wouldn't think of playing stickball in a park, ring-a-levio where there is shrubbery, or double-dutch on a grassy hillside. As another song tells us, "the great big city's a wondrous toy, just made for a girl and boy."

Pages 34-35

Fireworks are illegal in New York City, but the law is suspended in Chinatown during the four days of the first full moon after January 21, the Chinese New Year, known to Chinatown residents as the festival of Hsin Nien. The flying paper scraps from exploding firecrackers sometimes compete with snowflakes, as was the case when Kathy A. Yates aimed her camera down Mott Street in 1984.

Facing page

To provide a blow-by-blow description of the 1910 heavyweight championship fight between Jack Johnson and James J. Jeffreys, *The Times* installed an electric bulletin board on its headquarters building (Johnson won). Although it added the still-existing "zipper" sign with headline news encircling the building in time to announce Herbert Hoover's election as president in 1928 (Al Smith lost), the old bulletin board was still there in 1940 when Lou Stoumen took this picture he called "Sea of Hats." Like the sign, Nedicks orange drink, and roomy taxis, hats have vanished from the cityscape. The out-of-town newspaper stand is gone from 43rd Street, too.

Yesterday's newspaper is the only sign of "modern" times in Chaim Kanner's 1976 photograph of the Brooklyn Bridge pedestrian walkway. Cars and trucks are conveniently tucked away beneath the walkway, and except for the beehive sound they make—and the modern skyscrapers across the East River in Manhattan—a stroll over the bridge is very much as it was on May 24, 1883, when President Chester A. Arthur and future President Grover Cleveland led a ceremonial parade across the walkway from Manhattan and declared the independent cities of New York and Brooklyn united for the first time. Although the bridge physically united the two cities, it would be another fifteen years before they were politically merged to become Greater New York.

Facing page
When the Dutch created Nieuw Amsterdam at the tip of Manhattan Island, they wasted no time in trying to make it look like the old one and dug a wide canal from one end to the other. When the British took over, they filled in the canal and named it Broad Street. By 1919, when this picture was made of future financiers at the corner of Broad and Stone Streets, there was no trace of either the Dutch or the British, except possibly inside the Custom House at the end of the street, where sea captains paid their import taxes. Like Stone Street, most of Manhattan's streets were originally made of "cobblestones," which arrived here from Europe as ballast in sailing ships.

Facing page
The Main Concourse of Grand Central Terminal, shown here in about 1925 before the advertising community began adding its touches, is 160 feet by 470 feet, longer and wider than the nave of Notre Dame Cathedral. The ceiling is a plaster vault 150 feet high with a representation of the winter night sky punctuated by 2,500 electric lights representing the stars. Often called the "Crossroads of a Million Lives," Grand Central had its busiest year in 1947, when 65 million passengers passed through, a figure equal to 40 percent of the entire population of the United States at the time. In the mid-1940s, an average of 520 trains arrived or departed here every day of the week.

Pages 42-43
You can eat both lunch and dinner in a different New York restaurant every day for more than two years and never go to the same one twice. But you'd be hard-pressed to find a turkey dinner for a quarter, as you might have at this Woolworth lunch counter in 1942. Every Woolworth store in the city had a lunch counter back then, and some even had cafeterias.

Pages 44-45
During the years of peak immigration in the second half of the nineteenth century, most newcomers, especially the women, were forced to work in sweatshops, where they made clothing in unsafe surroundings at substandard wages. In 1911, fire engulfed the Triangle Shirtwaist Factory, and 146 workers, mostly Italian and Jewish immigrant girls, were killed. The tragedy brought about reforms in both safety and labor laws, but as Harvey Wang's recent image proves, sweatshops still exist in New York. They are concentrated in the Lower East Side, especially in the Chinatown area, where the current crop of workers is recruited from among Asian immigrants.

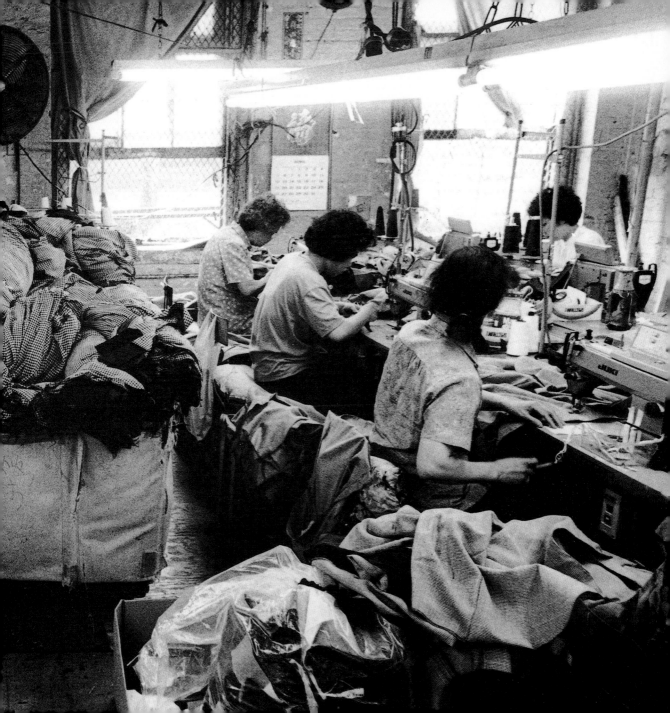

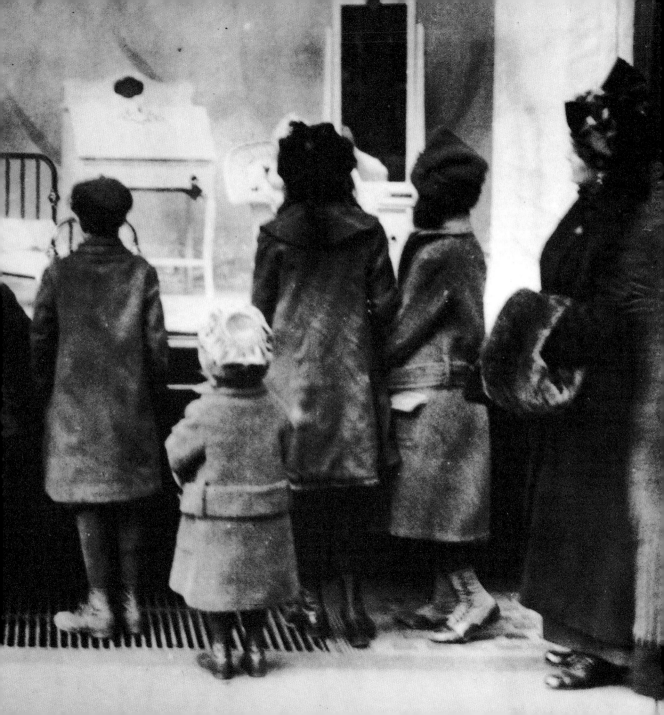

Pages 46-47

The store windows in New York are a window-shopper's dream, and all it takes is a few moments of your time to make a wish. The displays, like this one at Macy's in 1910, are especially beguiling at Christmastime. Often, New York's Christmas windows exclude merchandise and instead represent the retailer's wish for a happy holiday. That tradition began around the turn of the century when Lord & Taylor, in an effort to combat an unusually warm and un-Christmasy December, filled its windows with a simulated snowstorm to help shoppers get into the spirit of the season.

Because so many famous photographers have made studies of it, and because it is at the edge of the Photo District, the Flatiron Building is a kind of Mount Everest for New York photographers. Few have succeeded in capturing as arresting a view of it as

this one by Flo Fox, which she says she frequently signs at the top and the bottom because some people prefer to hang it upside down.

Facing page

Everything in Central Park is either man-made or was placed there by construction crews. The Pond at the southeast corner is no exception. The original plan by Frederick Law Olmstead and Calvert Vaux called for a nine-acre lake (reduced to five acres) to replace an existing swamp. The water came from an old mill stream that still flows under Fifth Avenue near 56th Street. When the park opened in 1858, swan boats plied the pond's waters. They disappeared in 1924, and ten years later, construction of a bridle path eliminated part of the pond itself. When the Wollman Memorial Skating Rink was added in 1951, two more acres of water disappeared. But if the pond isn't what it used to be, it is still a charming spot, as Chiam Kanner's photograph of it reveals.

Now called the Aquarium for Wildlife Conservation, the Coney Island outpost of the Bronx Zoo is the oldest public aquarium in the country. When opened to the public in 1902, it was housed at Castle Clinton in Manhattan's Battery Park. The present facility was built in 1955, a few blocks east along the Coney Island Boardwalk from Astroland and the Wonderwheel. The Aquarium also serves as a hospital for injured sea creatures that have been washed up on New York's beaches.

**After the 1840s, nearly
every private rowhouse
built in Manhattan was**
faced with a soft brown
sandstone quarried across
the river in New Jersey,
and before long the houses
became known as "brown-
stones." They all followed
the same basic architectur-
al plan—they were four
stories high, with a "stoop"
leading to the first floor
above ground level—and
might have looked exactly
the same except for the
fact that brownstone is soft
and was easily carved into
fanciful Greek-inspired
sculpture, used to accent
windows and doors.

**New Yorkers love nothing
better than talking, even if
the listener doesn't care**
what they have to say. Flo
Fox eavesdropped on such
a monologue one day in
Checker Park on Houston
Street near Sixth Avenue
and came away with this
image.

Facing page
**How many dogs are there in
New York City? Some days,
they seem to outnumber**
the people, and each and
every one of them, including this charmer smiling
for Chaim Kanner's cam-
era, has a personality all
its own.

Tonsorial art is not a spectator sport in New York, but every now and then, the client makes all the difference. Especially when it is broadcaster, newspaper columnist, lawyer, former congressman, best-selling author, and quintessential New Yorker Edward Irving Koch, who also served as the city's 105th mayor. A consummate politician, Koch can turn on a smile at the drop of a hat—but not for Harvey Wang's camera.

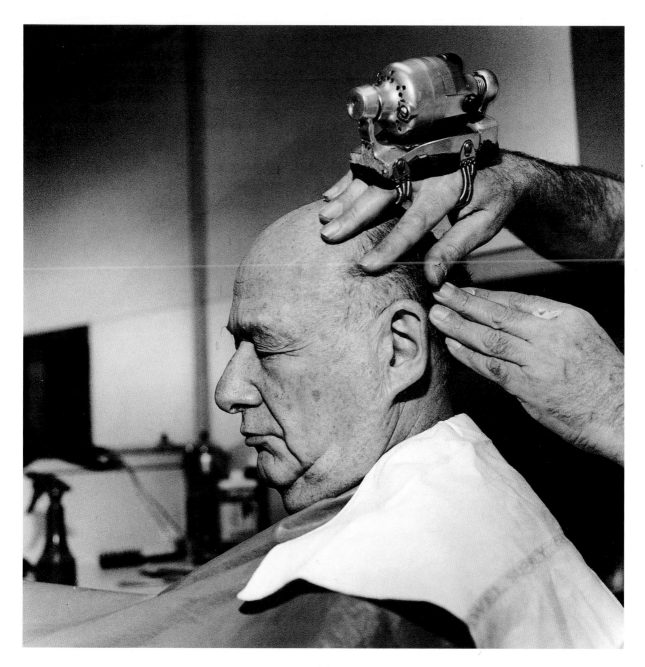

Although most unmarried New Yorkers protested with all the zeal of a philandering married man that they never went to singles bars, such places did a booming business in the 1960s and 1970s, even though, as Mary Ellen Mark's search for locations for the 1977 film *Looking for Mr. Goodbar* suggests, not every male customer got what he was looking for, as this fellow's forlorn expression suggests.

Facing page
More often than not, Manhattan's singles scene is a serious business, with tough competition always lurking in the background. Mary Ellen Mark found this young hopeful throwing caution to the wind by perching on a ladder. Did he get lucky? We'll never know. But as in every other form of hunting, most of the thrill comes from the chase itself. There is always another night, another bar, and, one hopes, less competition.

Jacqueline Kennedy Onassis was once a newspaper photographer herself, but she is camera-shy, and few candid shots of her exist. This one, taken in 1971, was a matter of great timing on the part of Ron Galella. "I saw Jackie walking up Fifth Avenue," he says, "and I hopped a cab to get in front of her. For once, Jackie's instincts were all wrong. Instead of turning away, she turned right toward me. This is my favorite photo of Jackie because it captures the qualities of the paparazzi style. The qualities are off-guard, spontaneous, and dramatic. Soft backlighting and composition show her at her sexiest. She is wearing no makeup and her hair is windblown, which adds up to real natural beauty. She turned around right after she heard the first click of my camera. After she discovered me, she put on her glasses and it was all over."

Facing page

Ron Galella spotted Woody Allen on Central Park West one day in 1988 leading Mia Farrow's daughter, Dylan, toward the Museum of Natural History. Like most New Yorkers, Woody is a consummate pedestrian. He has a chauffeur-driven car, but the driver usually just follows him around with the back seat empty. It comes in handy when he's in a hurry, of course, and think of the advantage if it should start to rain. At times like that, the rest of us are forced to buy a cheap umbrella from one of those sidewalk businesses that magically appear with the first drops.

Pages 60-61

Film crews never fail to attract crowds of curious onlookers, who stand in respectful silence for retake after retake. In this case, the crew was shooting a scene in *Sunday in New York* at Rockefeller Center's Channel Gardens.

Pages 62-63

After two months at the corner of Park Avenue and East 55th Street, Fernando Botero's massive sculpture *Roman Soldier* was hauled off to make way for the 1993 Christmas display in the Park Avenue malls. It was one of fourteen statues by the Colombian artist, most of them giant, bulbous nudes, that had been placed along the Avenue from 52nd to 61st Streets by the Public Art Fund. When they arrived, some Park Avenue doyennes protested, not because they objected to public nudity in their neighborhood, but that such a display would cause accidents among rubbernecking drivers. And while there was no increase in the accident rate, there was plenty of gawking by motorists and pedestrians.

Pages 64-65

One of the first things visitors notice about New York is that everybody always seems to be in a hurry. This is especially true in late fall, when more than 25,000 people from some 90 countries run as fast as they can for 26 miles, 385 yards, through all five boroughs in the annual New York City Marathon. The event began with 127 runners in 1970, and within 15 years it had become the world's largest marathon. Aid stations are set up every mile along the way to dispense cooling drinks. Add to that the friendly people who provide liquid refreshment as the runners pass through their neighborhoods, and the route becomes an obstacle course of discarded paper cups all the way from the Verrazano-Narrows Bridge in Staten Island to Central Park in Manhattan.

No, this isn't Frank Sinatra and Gene Kelly in a scene from *On the Town*, it's just a couple of your average gobs doing what sailors do best when the fleet's in. Harold Feinstein found them on the subway after a long, hard day at Coney Island on their way back to Manhattan for more adventure. Except for the Home Port on Staten Island, which is scheduled to close in 1994, there is no naval facility in New York harbor, although the city is a regular port of call for the U.S. Navy as well for fighting ships from just about every navy in the world. Was there ever a better place for a little R&R?

If you think all the bathing beauties are in Florida, think again. Harold Feinstein found plenty of bathers at Coney Island in 1951, and although styles have changed, you can still find them there any summer's day. In the beginning, the beach really was on an island, separated from the mainland by a creek extending east to Sheeps-head Bay. During a winter storm in 1839, the whole thing was washed out to sea, and a new beach was created, prompting an entrepreneur to build a toll road out of clam shells and put a hotel at the end, which he named the Coney Island House. Crowds have been flocking there ever since.

Some say that marriage is a roller-coaster existence. But not many of them start out that way, as did the marriage of Leslie Fratkin and David Lindsay in 1993, photographed by the already-wed Bob Krasner and Debra Trebitz. Leslie and David had just begun their life of wedded bliss as passengers aboard Coney Island's Cyclone. Beginning with the world's first roller coaster, the Switchback Railway, built at Coney Island in 1884, the list of Coney coasters has included the Thunderbolt, the Comet, the Rocket, and the Mile Sky Chaser. But the best of them all, in the opinion of most thrill-seekers, is the Cyclone, which has been operating since 1927.

Facing page
Back when he was a kid, and a ride on the Coney Island Cyclone cost ten cents, Harold Feinstein routinely spent all of his weekly entertainment budget by taking back-to-back trips on the roller coaster. "I was one of those crazy kids who always rode in the front car," he remembers, "and I always stood up for the downhill runs." By 1952, when he knew better than to stand up, Feinstein was still a front-car kind of guy. But by then he had a Leica to protect, and he used it to capture this shot of what he calls his "extended family" in the cars behind him.

Pages 72-73

The Brooklyn Dodgers were known to their fans as "the Flock," but they were also often called "the Bums" after losing the 1920 World Series. The Bums didn't win a pennant—and a chance to redeem themselves—again until 1941. But when they did, all of Brooklyn went bananas, hoisting beers in places like Fitzgerald's on Atlantic Avenue to toast manager Leo "the Lip" Durocher, as well as Dixie "Da People's Cherse" Walker, Pistol Pete Reiser, Pee Wee Reese, Dolf Camilli, Cookie Lavagetto, Whitlow Wyatt, and Billy Herman, among other stars who went on to (what else?) lose the Series. In 1957, the team picked up stakes and moved out west.

Facing page

New York isn't exactly at the heart of the snow belt, but around mid-February at least one major storm is likely. And it doesn't take much of the white stuff to shut the city down. This 1978 storm brought things to a halt outside McGowan's Bar at Perry Street and Greenwich Avenue, and by early evening, when Harold Feinstein happened by, nearly everybody was inside talking about the weather but not really doing much about it. The tall structure in the background was St. Vincent's Hospital on Seventh Avenue.

Pages 76-77

Much of what Todd Webb saw when he photographed the downtown skyline from the Empire State Building in 1946 is still there, including the Con Edison and the Metropolitan Life towers with their giant clocks. Fifth Avenue, in the center foreground, has hardly changed a bit; nor has Broadway veering off to the left past the Flatiron Building. Another difference from then to now is that only one building in the panorama is floodlit (except for 70 Pine Street, off in the distance), which is what you would expect of the Con Edison Building. It *is* the electric company, after all.

"This guy went to the same school I did," says Sid Kaplan, **"and one Saturday night** in 1951, I spotted him asleep on the IRT Lexington Avenue Local, and I nailed him." With his camera, of course. Sid says his former schoolmate is a prominent architect today and probably doesn't sleep on the subway any longer. The girlfriend? "I don't remember her name," says the photographer. "I'm not sure I ever knew it. We just called her 'the cute little redhead'." New York's is still the only rapid transit system in the world that will get you where you want to go 24 hours a day, 365 days a year. And no other system gets you there as fast or takes you as far for a single fare.

CREDITS AND SOURCES

Text: Bill Harris

Series Editor: J.C. Suarès

Photo Editor: Leslie Fratkin

Design: Lisa Lytton-Smith